Too Cute!

Baby Pigs

by Elizabeth Neuenfeldt

BELLWETHER MEDIA
MINNEAPOLIS, MN

BLASTOFF!
Beginners

Blastoff! Beginners are developed by literacy experts and educators to meet the needs of early readers. These engaging informational texts support young children as they begin reading about their world. Through simple language and high frequency words paired with crisp, colorful photos, Blastoff! Beginners launch young readers into the universe of independent reading.

Blastoff! Universe ★

Reading Level — Grade K (Blastoff! Beginners)
Grades 1-3 (Blastoff! Readers)
Grade 4 (Blastoff! Discovery)

Sight Words in This Book 🔍

all	get	on	these
and	have	other	they
are	her	play	this
at	in	run	to
big	look	the	up
eat	many	them	

This edition first published in 2023 by Bellwether Media, Inc.

No part of this publication may be reproduced in whole or in part without written permission of the publisher. For information regarding permission, write to Bellwether Media, Inc., Attention: Permissions Department, 6012 Blue Circle Drive, Minnetonka, MN 55343.

Library of Congress Cataloging-in-Publication Data

LC record for Baby Pigs available at: https://lccn.loc.gov/2022036375

Text copyright © 2023 by Bellwether Media, Inc. BLASTOFF! BEGINNERS and associated logos are trademarks and/or registered trademarks of Bellwether Media, Inc.

Editor: Betsy Rathburn   Designer: Jeffrey Kollock

Printed in the United States of America, North Mankato, MN.

Table of Contents

A Baby Pig!

Look at the
baby pig.
Hello, piglet!

On the Farm

Piglets live on farms. They sleep in **pens**.

pen

Piglets stay close to mom. They drink her milk.

Piglets have
many **siblings**.
They love
to cuddle!

siblings

Piglets play.
They run
and push.

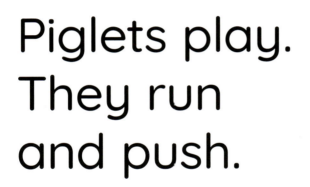

They roll
in mud.
This keeps
them cool!

Farmers give piglets **feed**. They eat corn and other plants.

feed

Growing Up

Piglets grow.
They get
very big!

These piglets are all grown up.
Bye, mom!

Baby Pig Facts

Pig Life Stages

piglet   adult

A Day in the Life

play   roll in mud   eat feed

Glossary

feed

pig food made from corn and other plants

pens

homes for pigs

siblings

brothers and sisters

To Learn More

ON THE WEB

FACTSURFER

Factsurfer.com gives you
a safe, fun way to find
more information.

1. Go to www.factsurfer.com.

2. Enter "baby pigs" into the search box
   and click $\mathcal{Q}$.

3. Select your book cover to see a list
   of related content.

Index

The images in this book are reproduced through the courtesy of: Eric Isselee, front cover, pp. 1, 4, 10; Tsekhmister, pp. 3, 5, 22 (piglet); JLWhitePhotography, p. 6; Kenishirotie, pp. 6-7; yevgeniy11, pp. 8-9; Brenda Bakker, pp. 10-11; photomaster, p. 12; Christine Louise, pp. 12-13; Ernie Janes/ Alamy, pp. 14-15; Dusan Petkovic, pp. 16-17; sapegin, pp. 18-19; Photolines, pp. 20-21; Olga_i, p. 22 (adult); Juniors Bildarchiv GmbH/ Alamy, p. 22 (play); Warren Parker, p. 22 (mud); apidach, p. 22 (eat); CHIRATH PHOTO, p. 23 (feed); MicrostockStudio, p. 23 (pens); HQuality, p. 23 (siblings).